"In *Where Do I Come From?*, Father Paul offers us a profound blessing . . . an invitation to 'come and see.' It is an invitation to journey with Jesus and to experience his deep love and healing presence in our lives today."

—**JOHN RICE**, director, The Blessing
Place of Western North Carolina

"What is our true identity? . . . Our true identity is to live and remain in Christ. Once we begin to live this out, our lives are set free. It's hard not to read this book and sense that God wants to do some inner spiritual cleaning and healing in our relationships. . . . I encourage you to read this book and ask the Holy Spirit to guide, heal, and restore you to your true identity."

—**TODD MCGREGOR**, SAMS Missionary

"In his truly winsome fashion, Feider has written a gem of a book that takes the revelation of Jesus Christ into a deeply personal conversation about our own hearts. This book is a guide to our interior life where we seek healing. The journey takes us from anxiety, shame, unforgiveness, and traumatic memories to a new life and destiny based on our identity in Christ. If you desire a deeper intimacy with God, this is the book for you."

—**JUDITH MACNUTT**, cofounder and
president, Christian Healing Ministries

"Father Paul has a mild, reassuring manner that blends well with his piercing devotion to the healing ministry. He has a way of quickly going to the heart of a problem and is a master at simplifying complicated situations. In this book, Father Paul walks us through John's Gospel to help us find inner peace, joy, and contentment."

—**MALCOLM SELF**, board of directors,
International Order of St. Luke the Physician

"With biblical insight taken from John's Gospel and pastoral care learned from a life of service, Paul Feider has written an important book about identity and a purposeful life from a Christian viewpoint. His insights to healing from past pain, trauma, low self-esteem, depression, and anxiety in this book is an effective guide in discovering our life as God's children and Christ's servants. The helpful questions in each section invite the reader into a deeper and more meaningful life."

—KEVIN MARTIN, teacher and author

Where Do I Come From?

Where Do I Come From?

My True Identity

PAUL FEIDER

RESOURCE *Publications* · Eugene, Oregon

WHERE DO I COME FROM?
My True Identity

Resource Publications
An Imprint of Wipf and Stock Publishers
199 W. 8th Ave., Suite 3
Eugene, OR 97401

www.wipfandstock.com

PAPERBACK ISBN: 978-1-6667-4250-3
HARDCOVER ISBN: 978-1-6667-4251-0
EBOOK ISBN: 978-1-6667-4252-7

05/12/22

Thank you, Donna Self and Laura Sinclair for
your help in making this book possible.

Contents

Introduction

What is my true identity? How do I perceive myself? Do I have within me a deep inner joy because of who I am? The way we answer these questions effects the way we live and can even limit our vision of life. Do I identify myself as coming from a certain family, or from a certain ethnic background? Do I perceive myself as from a good home, broken home, or a dysfunctional family? Do I see myself as a leader, a follower, as not good enough, or as one better than most people? Do I identify myself by my occupation: a nurse, a school teacher, a truck drive, a factory worker, a pastor, a waiter? We may be one or the other of these things, but what is my true identity? From where do I get my self-worth, my energy, and purpose? Where do I really come from and where am I ultimately going?

To delve into these deeper questions, we might want to take a closer look at the gospel of John. It gives an account of the life of Jesus but it does much more than that. It allows us to know the events of Jesus' life, but it also draws us into the deeper meaning of those events to reveal Jesus' true identity and discover our own true identity. It challenges us to make a spiritual journey into the life of Jesus so that we might discover the peace, the security with which Jesus lived. That discovery maps the path for a life of true peace, clear direction, inner security, abundant joy, and eternal relationship. In addition, this journey allows us to find our true identity in God. If such a life interests you, I suggest we keep walking together into the deeper message found in the gospel of John and the fruits of living the life we were created to live.

Where Do I Come From?

We believe that the scriptures are inspired by God which means they are flowing with the Holy Spirit of God. When we take time to soak in the gospels, we not only learn about Jesus but we can experience his Spirit flowing through the words and interacting with our spirit to bring about transformation and healing. This book is about soaking in the deeper-inspired message found in the gospel of John, one that can enhance our lives and heal us within.

We will begin with examining some passages in John's gospel which offer answers to these deeper questions of life: What is my true identity? How do I identify myself? Where do I really come from, and where am I ultimately going? I will highlight certain words because John does a play on words to invite us to reflect on where we come from and where we are going. He suggests the double meaning of certain words to draw us into an important aspect of Jesus' message. This spiritual reflection builds off the word **"where"** or "*pothen*" in Greek. We will look at his use of the word "where" to reflect on our true identity and the healing power of an encounter with Jesus. John also uses words like "see," "remain," "know" and "believe into" as a means of drawing us into an experience of the transforming power of being with Jesus. We will let these words resonate within us as we make this spiritual journey.

This journey can be made alone, but it may have a greater life-changing effect if it is made with another person or group of people seeking a richer, more meaningful life. This book is not designed to be read quickly but rather savored, allowing the thoughts and questions to refashion our self-perception. It may also help us rethink some misguided views of ourselves and heal from the effects of those views. The *questions* at the ends of the chapters invite some deep sharing and new discoveries. The *prayers* empower us to release and heal wounded memories and hidden feelings that keep us from living the fullness of life as God intended. The *practical applications* can help us practice new ways of thinking and acting as we seek to live our true identity.

Chapter 1

Where Do You Stay?

The next day John was there again with two of his disciples. As he watched Jesus walk by he said, "Look! There is the Lamb of God! The two disciples heard what he said, and followed Jesus. When Jesus turned around and noticed them following him, he asked them, "What are you looking for?" They said to him, "Rabbi (which means teacher), where do you stay?" "Come and see," he answered. So, they went to see where he was lodged, and stayed with him that day.

JOHN 1:35-39

REFLECTION

This passage in the early part of John's gospel offers us questions to begin our spiritual journey. "What are your looking for?" is Jesus' question to the disciples, and it is also our question. What am I looking for in life? What do I really desire? Where am I headed? What is the ultimate goal and purpose of my life? If those questions have truly meaningful answers, we must ask the disciples' question to Jesus, namely, where do you stay? If we wish to know our true identity, our real origin, and our ultimate destiny, we must spend time with our Creator and discover where he stays.

When the disciples ask Jesus where he stays, there is no physical place mentioned to answer that question. There are no physical directions given. There is only the short answer, "Come and see." To discover where Jesus stayed meant that the disciples had to move out of where they were and go to where Jesus was. This move not only meant a walk to his house but, more importantly, an inner movement in their hearts to discover where Jesus "stayed," where his heart found rest and purpose.

This is the challenge for us. If we wish to discover where Jesus stays, we must choose to search. The double meaning of "Come and see" challenges us as readers to choose to open our eyes, our minds, our hearts, and ponder where we are relative to Jesus and how we can discover the inner peace that he had. Where do we stay relative to where Jesus stays? Are we willing to "come and see?" Do we want to honestly "know" him and our true identity? If we tasted of his love, would we "believe into" him and perhaps eventually "remain" with him? These are all the questions that arise as we seek deep inner peace and our real purpose in life. These are the questions John raises for us as we explore his gospel. In the end his words offer a rich promise about the only place to live, the most enjoyable place to "stay."

John begins his gospel in this way: "In the beginning was the Word and the Word was in God's presence, and the Word was God." This first line of the gospel tells us that "the Word, Jesus, was with God, the Father. As the gospel goes on, Jesus will remind us that he is in the Father and the Father is in him. That is where he "stays" during his life on earth. That is his identity. That is his source of power. That is his connection and his reality from which he teaches and heals. Even though we are not God, we are children of God and can live in the joy and serenity of being with God. Our identity comes from our Creator. If we have lost our true identity, Jesus invites us to "come and see" where he stays so that we can choose to stay there also. He wants to restore our vision of ourselves so that we can live as the Father intended us to live.

The real question you want to ponder is, "Where do *you* stay; that is, where is the place from which you think and feel?" From what place do you live every day? Where is your mind during the day? Where is your heart? What is your perception of yourself relative to God's purpose for your life?

Maybe you "stay" in your head, perhaps to avoid feeling pain, perhaps to avoid feeling the memories of long ago, perhaps to fulfill your dream of making money or getting recognition. Maybe you "stay" in your wounded heart and keep reliving the pain of traumatic memories. Maybe you "stay" in the past because it was better than your present situation. Maybe you "stay" in the grasp of shame or low self-esteem, and it clouds your true identity. Maybe you "stay" bound by worry or anxiety, fear or sadness, anger or unforgiveness. Life can be challenging at times, and it is not always fair. This passage gives us hope. Jesus said, "Come and see." If we step out of our inner life and take time to come and see where Jesus lives, then we can experience his love for us and his power to transform our lives. We can take steps to "stay" where Jesus stays, to heal and find that place of inner serenity.

John uses the word "where" to invite us to reflect on our choices in life and our decision about Jesus. It is one of the most significant words in Johns' gospel because our joy and meaning in life are about where we live relative to where Jesus lives. Some of us may have a bad impression of Jesus because of our religious training or lack of it. We may not be interested in Jesus, but then the questions become, "Do we like where we stay? Do we live every day with serenity and inner peace? Do we wake up with joy in our hearts that sustains us throughout the day? If not, then Jesus' response to the disciples may offer us hope, "Come and see."

Jesus stayed in the Father's love. He invites us to "Come and see" what that life is like. We do not have to live in pain, or the past, or in fear, or shame, or anger. Where we "stay "mentally, emotionally, and spiritually is our choice. We may not always understand it as a choice, but it is. Whatever our past has been, we can be set free and healed. The invitation is there for us to "come and see," to experience a new vision of life.

What does that mean for us? It means we can begin a new journey. We can decide to come out of where we are "staying" and discover that life can be much better. That journey may begin with reading through this gospel and taking time to ponder Jesus' deep love for us. It might start by talking with someone who knows the heart of Jesus and asking them to help us feel Jesus' love throughout our whole life story.

The journey to a new, freer life might take us back into our past to uncover the source of our hurt, shame, fear, or anger and then discover Jesus' presence there because he was there. This process is what we call inner healing. I have helped people for over 40 years to heal from the wounded emotions connected to past memories. When they were intentionally ready to go back to the painful memories, identify Jesus' presence there, and then receive his love for them in that moment, their painful feelings were released, and they found a new inner peace. They could begin each day from a new place of serenity. They lived; they "stayed" in a new place because they came to see Jesus in their story. They saw themselves in a new light because life changes when we invite Jesus to walk with us and open our eyes to our true identity. The more we see and feel Jesus in our story, the more likely we can arrive at that place of divine serenity where Jesus stayed.

To discover this new place to stay, we need to come out of our old place. If we bury ourselves in our phone, computer, or television, we may need to turn them off and find a new source for life-fulfilling information. We do not have to stay there. If we medicate our feelings with alcohol, food, or other drugs, we will need to name the real issue and invite Jesus to heal this core issue that causes our compulsion to medicate. It may not be easy to let go of our securities and hiding places unless we know there is a better place where we can find serenity. Jesus offers us that place if we will "come and see" where he stays and release our pain into his hands. It is often helpful to find a healthy person to walk with us as we make this healing transition, and we might seek out someone who is making the journey to freedom themselves.

We may be living each day imprisoned in wounded emotions. If we live in continual fear or anxiety, taking Jesus to the core source of the feelings will lessen them and eventually set us free of them. We may need to find someone with whom we can express our feelings and who is able to pray with us as we invite Jesus into the core wound. If we are willing to step through our initial fear, go back to the core wound, and receive Jesus' love in that place, we will discover a deep peace and new courage for the next challenge. Having someone with us who knows the heart of Jesus can help us make this healing journey.

If the place from which we think and feel is controlled by a strong, "shame voice" inside us that limits our life or ministry, we need to "come and see" Jesus and what he has to say about us. Jesus would never shame us, and his voice of our true identity dispels the lie of the "shame voice." We can see Jesus stand between us and the voice of a shaming parent or significant person in our life. By Jesus' power, we can forgive the person who shamed us and then let the voice of Jesus replace the "shame voice" we internalized. Jesus offers us the true voice about ourselves, and this truth will set us free. Healing of our "shame voice" changes our view of ourselves, affecting our identity. We no longer think of ourselves as not good enough, unworthy, or a mistake but we see ourselves as precious and holy as God sees us.

If we feel unworthy or not good enough, then we are invited to break the power of that false voice by listening to the true voice of Jesus regarding our value and worthiness. We can listen to his voice of affirmation and assurance that God loves us dearly and would never think of us as unworthy. Then we can live each day from a place of emotional, mental, and spiritual serenity. Coming into this new place of freedom takes some continual effort and letting go of the old voice, but it is worth it. Living in the constant affirming voice of Jesus is the treasured place to "stay." It is helpful to begin hanging out with people who live in this treasured place.

Where Do I Come From?

We do not have to stay in a prison of excessive fear or anxiety, anger or shame. We can experience freedom by inviting in Jesus' healing presence. We do not have to be limited by our inaccurate thoughts or wounded memories but can meet each day aware that we are a beloved child of the Creator. We can enter relationships and take on new challenges with confidence that we have a God who loves us and has an eternal purpose for our lives. Taking time to "come and see" Jesus in our story offers us a new view of life.

We each have experienced losses in our lives, and if we never learned how to grieve them, they can accumulate. As each new loss is added, the pain and sadness can be overwhelming. Life can seem difficult. It does not have to be. We can invite Jesus to be with us in our grief, to cry with us, and to offer us the hope of his resurrection. The story of the raising of Lazarus in chapter 11 of John's gospel tells us that Jesus cried with Mary and Martha at the death of their brother. Feeling Jesus with us in our times of loss and knowing that he understands can help us release the sadness and discover the promise of new life that Jesus gives. Like Mary and Martha, we open the tombs of our life with Jesus and discover the new life he can bring from any loss. There is a spark of resurrection in every loss and we experience it when we "come and see" where Jesus is in the loss and listen for his voice. Having someone with us as we process the losses in our life is a great help in releasing the pain and moving forward in peace.

We may be staying in an emotional place of unforgiveness. Sometimes people hurt us quite deeply, and there is a temptation to retaliate. We need to have a place to express our hurt and anger, but there is a time to forgive. Jesus offered people forgiveness and forgave people who hurt him. On the cross, he prayed for those who crucified him, saying, "Father, forgive them for they do not know what they are doing." He lived and stayed in a place of serenity by releasing any unforgiveness.

The desire for revenge or the will to punish someone actually hurts us. Choosing not to forgive someone does not hurt them, but it holds us in an emotional prison and locks out any hope of healing. It only harms us. It tears at our body and lessens our immune system. If we live in a place of unforgiveness, Jesus invites us to "come and see" where he stays and discover how he was able to forgive. We can feel his generous mercy toward us and discover the freedom of offering forgiveness to those who hurt us. We can "stay" in the place of inner peace where Jesus lived. I have helped many people give the gift of forgiveness by praying a prayer of blessing for the offender. The choice to forgive and pray this prayer set them free. It released their anger and gave them new energy to move forward in peace. It also allowed them to feel deeply the forgiveness Jesus had given to them. This inner serenity is available to us.

The way we live our lives has all to do with where we stay, the place from which we think and feel. It is a relief to know that we do not have to stay in an unhealthy place in life. No one can keep us there but ourselves. Our inner life is of our own making, and Jesus offers us the power to live in freedom, peace, and joy. There are stories of people who lived through the concentration camps with inner peace. I listened to people in Uganda who had almost nothing and had many family members killed in wars, but they had a peace about them that came from their relationship with Jesus. They had a joy not because life was fair or they were free of pain but because they were in love with their Maker. No one could take that away.

The last line of this section leaves us another important clue as to what changed these disciples' lives. It says, "So they went to see where Jesus stayed and remained with him that day." The word "remain" is significant in life transformation. Remaining with Jesus gave the disciples time to ingest his words, his care, his compassion, his love, which would gradually draw them out of their old place to live the life of true freedom. I have ministered to many people who learned how to "remain" with Jesus every day. They would begin each day in quiet reflection and prayer, worshiping God and inviting Jesus to walk with them throughout the day. Many saw gradual inner healings happen in their life through months of weekly worship in our community. They "remained" close to Jesus, absorbing his love. Their lives became more and more peaceful as they experienced his love and the inner healing power of that love.

I have also known many people who came to know Jesus at some point in their life and even experienced inner healing but then did not remain. They got pulled back into their old world to stay where they used to be instead of in the presence of Jesus. Their fears came back, their "shame voice" controlled them again, unforgiveness crept in, along with a low-level anger. They began to worry and be stressed again. They lost the joy in life they experienced when they first came to know Jesus and feel his love for them. As we continue this journey, we will look at the treasure of "remaining" with Jesus and the things that keep us connected.

PRAYER

Jesus, thank you for coming to earth and showing us a way to discover who we really are in your eternal plan. I desire to know my true identity and the power of your love for me. I want to see myself as you see me and become the person your saw in me when your created me. I want to be free of the thoughts and feeling that hold me back from a life of joy and inner peace. I want to "come and see" you in a deeper way and remain with you each day.

Jesus, I pray now that I might hear and accept your invitation to "come and see" the life that I can have in you. Heal me of my past wounded memories causing unnecessary fear, anxiety, resentments, and shame that hinder my life. Walk through my whole life so that I might feel your loving, healing presence all the way back to my conception. Release from my memory the weight of anything that keeps me from living my true identity. Help me to forgive from my heart any person who was part of creating those harmful memories. Take me deeper into your heart so that I may feel the heart of your Father in heaven. Give me the Peace that only you can give. Thank you for hearing me and loving me. Thank you for inviting me to come and experience the life of wholeness and true peace.

QUESTIONS FOR REFLECTION/DISCUSSION

1. Where do you stay emotionally?

2. Where to you stay mentally?

3. Where do you hide so as not to feel?

4. What would you be willing to change to "come and see" a new way of living?

5. How might you "remain" with Jesus?

PRACTICAL APPLICATION

Slowly read through chapters 14–17 of John's gospel, being attentive to Jesus' deep love.

CHAPTER 2

Where Do You Come From?

Jesus spoke to them once again. "I am the light of the world. No follower of mine shall ever walk in darkness; no, he shall possess the light of life."

This caused the Pharisees to break in with: "You are your own witness. Such testimony cannot be valid." Jesus answered: "What if I am my own witness? My testimony is valid nonetheless, because I know where I came from and where I am going."

JOHN 8:12–14

Jesus said, "The Father already loves you, because you have loved me and have believed that I came from God. I did indeed come from the Father; I came into the world. Now I am leaving the world to go to the Father."

JOHN 16:27–28

REFLECTION

Before we look at the other reflections on the word "where," we want to examine Jesus' most profound statement about his origin and destiny. In John 8:14, he says, "I know where I came from and where I am going." His security to speak and minister as Abba Father directed came from knowing his origin and destiny. He lived his whole life in a conscious love relationship with Abba. He expresses this clearly when he says, "I came from the Father and entered the world; now I am leaving the world and going back to the Father" (John 16:28). His power to heal flowed from that deep, love relationship. His authority to teach came from that connection. His inner security to stand before Pilate and tell him, "You would have no power over me whatever unless it were given you from above" (John 19:11), gave witness to his divine relationship. His mission to carry out all that the Father asks made sense because he knew where he came from and where he was going. This is the treasure of knowing his origin and his destiny.

The whole gospel goes on to describe people who knew where Jesus was from and those who did not. To know they had to "come and see"; they had to let go of their old mindset and enter the mindset of Jesus. Jesus says to the Pharisees, after he describes his origin and destiny, that they know neither of these. They think they know where he came from, namely, that he came from Galilee, but their knowledge blinds them to the deeper truth. The word used here for "know" (*iodate* in Greek) means to know in one's head from human resources like we know the pull of gravity.

John does an interesting play on words regarding knowing Jesus' origin. In chapter seven, he records a whole discussion of Jesus' origins. The people of Jerusalem said, "We know where this man is from. When the Messiah comes, no one is supposed to know his origins" (John 7:27). What they thought they knew distracted them from seeking to "know" Jesus. They knew something about Jesus, but they did not "know" him. In John 10:14, Jesus says, "I know my sheep and my sheep know me." This type of "knowing" (*ginosko* in Greek) is to know in the heart, be connected, be ready to remain with, listen to and follow.

The religious leaders did not know Jesus because they did not "come and see." Their study and learning could only take them so far. At some point, they had to look into Jesus' eyes and feel this deep love. Their human knowledge kept them from opening to a deep heart encounter with Jesus. They did not want to let go of their presuppositions about the Messiah, and they did not want to follow what Jesus taught. Their training had locked them into a certain worldview, and they were not willing to surrender that view for a larger, divine worldview. They thought they knew, but they did not know. Knowing Jesus means an opening of the heart and mind, entering into a relationship that may go in an unknown direction. It involves letting go and it may involve sacrifice or ridicule. If they felt secure in their worldview, it was challenging to step into a new perspective and follow Jesus.

These religious leaders also would have had to change some of their practices which they felt were important. They had Sabbath practices which they felt were more important than healing a man who was crippled. Their training in worldly knowledge blinded them to knowing Jesus and coming to see who he really was. John does a fascinating play on words in chapter nine about the religious leaders' blindness and the blind man who could see. The blind man was able to see Jesus because he listened to Jesus' voice, obeyed what Jesus asked him to do, and let go of his old way of doing things. He was willing to surrender his understanding of the old law once he saw who Jesus really was. He knew then that he knew, and no one could take that away from him. He said, "Once I was blind, but now I see." He no longer identified himself as one born in sin but rather saw himself as a disciple of Jesus, who opened his eyes. He was a new person. His perception of his origin changed, so his perception of his destiny changed. He was going to hold onto his new vision and new identity, even if it meant being thrown out of his church. He now saw who he was, and he was not letting go of the One who gave him this new sight.

Sometimes, today's religious leaders have a harder time accepting Jesus' love than others because they have invested in a certain view or theology. Their head knowledge can make it harder to let go and allow Jesus' love to break into their heart, even though deep down their heart yearns to be set free. I have seen this in my peers through my years in ministry. Ironically, most of our training to be pastors does not teach us how to surrender and allow God to direct our lives. It does not lead us to discover where we came from and where we are going. It does not help us to experience God's personal love for us and the miracles that happen when we live our lives in the power of that love. We are sometimes taught to distrust our emotions and the healing power of God's intense love. We are taught about Jesus but often not invited to experience the heart of Jesus and the treasure of a personal relationship with him.

I have also known religious leaders who have stepped through their fears, let go of presuppositions, and discovered a whole new way of living in the Presence. They have allowed their hearts to feel the love that created them, the love that redeemed them, the love that heals them. They know a new power and energy in their ministry. They speak with the authority that comes from being connected to the Master. They see healings happen when they minister the love of Jesus to people. They walk through ridicule with their eyes fixed on Jesus. They exude an inner peace that is contagious. They know where they come from and where they are going.

Earthly head knowledge can block us from knowing the heart of Jesus. When I was in college training for ministry, a priest invited me to a retreat about Jesus' love and the Holy Spirit. I had grown up in a religious home, studied the Bible and felt that I knew Jesus. I told the priest I did not need that retreat. The priest was gentle, but he invited me to "come and see." I did go, and after listening to his reflection and taking quiet extended time to listen for the voice of Jesus, I "saw" Jesus in a new way. I felt his love like never before and could not stop reading his life story in the gospels. I went from knowing about him to "knowing" him. He became my trusted friend. That made all the difference in my life. From then on, I was connected to him in a new way and I was determined to live as he directed. I went from telling him what I needed when I prayed to listening to what he needed from me. Feeling his love every day healed the wounded places in my story that needed to be healed. Knowing Jesus' Presence filled me with inner security and peace as I approached ministry. This opened a whole new way of viewing life and empowered me to offer God's healing love to thousands of people for the past fifty years.

I discovered in the gospel that those who knew Jesus in this way knew where he came from and where he was going. They knew because they let go of their earthly mindset and put on the mind of Jesus. They came to know the deeper truth about who he really was. This knowledge gave their lives new meaning and purpose. It gave them clarity about what is important. It gave them a sense of self-worth they did not have before. This is evident when we read Peter's bold statement to Jesus as people were walking away. Jesus asked the disciples, "Do you want to leave me too?" Peter answered, "Lord, to whom shall we go? You have the words of eternal life. We have come to believe; we are convinced that you are God's holy one" (John 6:67–69). He had given up his shameful view of himself and received Jesus' view of him as a leader. He had given up where he usually "stayed," his old emotional place from which he lived, and began remaining with Jesus. His knowledge of Jesus' heart and values drew him into a relationship worth dying for. He knew where he came from, so he was not afraid of following Jesus no matter where it took him. He could live life with deep inner security that no one could take away. He was not going to give up that treasure.

Peter and the apostles came to know that Jesus came from the Father and was going back to the Father. Gradually they would learn that they also came from the Father and that they were going back to the Father. Jesus taught them how to live, explaining that he only does what the Father tells him, that he speaks as the Father directs (John 7:16). Once they knew their real origin and destiny, they lived with new purpose, courage, and security. They were directed by a new voice. They were "born from above." As long as they remained with Jesus, they could do the works he did because they knew the power came from above, from the Father's love. Even after his resurrection, they felt his holy love, his Holy Spirit empowering their ministry. The relationship continued.

Knowing where Jesus came from and where he is going is very significant for our spiritual journey and it invites us to answer the most significant questions of life, namely, where do you come from, and where are you going?

When people ask you, "Where do you come from?" what do you say? You may often name the city where you grew up or, depending on the circumstances, name the state you are from or your country of origin. But the spiritual journey on which John takes us challenges us to dig deeper. It is all about the "where" questions. Where do I come from, and where am I going?

This gospel challenges me to examine my inner dialogue to determine the interior place where I make decisions about myself and others. What are my thoughts and feelings about myself from which I speak and act? What dominates my thoughts and feelings, and what are my values in light of my origins? Then there is the question, "Where am I going?" What is my direction or purpose in life? What is my mission, and what is the goal? What choices do I make in light of my origin and destiny? Where do I come from, and where am I going? These are the spiritual questions that determine our behavior and feelings about ourselves and others. We take a moment to ponder these questions.

Sometimes I talk with people who have very low self-esteem. I ask them where they came from, and they will describe a family of origin with no affirmation but only many shaming words. They were told that they would never amount to anything or that they were not smart enough. If they desire healing and freedom from the shaming voice that has held them back, I invite them to go back to the time before they did anything or anything was done to them. We walk back into the center of the Father, the Son and the Holy Spirit, where they were loved into existence, where they were conceived. We take time to sit in the beauty of that perfect love and hear the Creator say to them, "You are my beloved daughter, my beloved son, on you my favor rests." As they soak in this environment, the divine voice of love gets stronger than the voice of shame that came after it. They realize that the divine voice is the truth about them, and the later shaming voice is the lie. Once they reflect on where they came from, their view of themselves changes. The true voice dispels the lie and heals the wounds it caused. They are more prepared to step into their purpose in life with a sense of value. Knowing where they came from opens the door to discover where they are destined to go. These people realize the divine Presence has been with them all along and will be with them to the end. They experience deep joy and start to live as they were intended to live. They no longer think of themselves as coming from a shame-based home or dysfunctional family, but rather from the perfect love in the center of the Trinity. Like Jesus, they can say, "I came from the Father, and I am going back to the Father." That path is surrounded by peace, joy, and serenity. They have a new identity.

This inner healing journey works because God's love was there before anything else and has been there all along. It works because we each have a divine origin and a divine destiny. Knowing this may have gotten lost in the human woundedness of our environment, but it remains and can be discovered. This is the message and the healing power that Jesus brought into the world. It is accessible to all who "come and see," all who are willing to move out of their present place to the place where Jesus is. That is the message of Jesus recorded in John's gospel. It's all about "where" we live, the place from which we approach life. It is about how we view ourselves, about knowing our true origin and destiny.

Other feelings also respond to the creative love that is available to us. People may have experienced a traumatic event early in life or grew up in an environment where they never felt safe. They live with constant anxiety, which seems to have been there for their whole life. They recall being afraid when they were very young. If they had a traumatic event and continue to live in its fearful effects, I walk back with them to the time of the event and invite them to feel Jesus' presence there. I invite them to go back to their origin when they were loved into existence by God. As they take time to feel the divine presence throughout their story and particularly during the traumatic event, the fear and anxiety begin to lessen. It may take some time, but their life begins to become more peaceful and secure as they often soak in the holy presence that created them. If they never felt safe as a child, they can begin to feel safe in their present state in life because they have chosen to accept Jesus' love and security in their life. They can know true serenity. This works because they came from the Father, and they are going back to the Father. Knowing that reality makes all the difference.

Some people will say they come from an alcoholic home or an abusive home. If they did not get the nurture and love they needed, they now live with deep pain and emptiness. Sometimes they have little hope of a better life. Jesus' message and his presence can free them from the pain of their situation. I invited many of them to feel the Creator's love before they did anything and before anything was done to them. If they take time to rest in the love of the Father, Son, and Holy Spirit where they were conceived, they begin to have the energy to release all the pain from the things that were done to them. They realize that they were loved into existence, and the same love could heal them of the wounds they experienced in life. The love of God fills in all the empty places where they did not feel loved during their life. The memories of abuse and neglect give way to the memories of being surrounded by perfect love. They experience a new joy and serenity. Often, they become effective ministers of healing for others with the same background.

Even if we feel that we came from a loving home, discovering the larger picture of our life opens us to new possibilities. We may feel good about ourselves and have a certain security. Still, maybe we do not have the many spiritual gifts and the healing energy that is available to us for handling the challenges of life. We all face some difficult times, and realizing that we have a divine presence with us can make the difference between being stressed and at peace. We all face times when we get afraid of the next step in life. Being aware of the Father's continual creative love surrounding us empowers us to walk through these times with courage and inner peace. Knowing where we come from and where we are going allows us to see God-moments every day. It gives us a sense of purpose, an excitement about where God is taking us on this divine journey. It frees us of the need to have all the answers since we know that our Creator knows them. It opens us to the miracles available to us if we only ask and receive. It is a way of living what Jesus calls the "fullness of life" John 10:10).

This whole journey brings comfort to the times in life when we face losses. We all experience losses of friendships, family connections, losses of health, and losses through death. These are not easy times, but if we know our origin and destiny, then all of these things feel different. If we live in the bigger picture of Jesus' love surrounding us at all times, we can walk through these times with a sense of peace. We can cry, but we feel Jesus crying with us. At the death of a loved one, we have the promise that we will see them again because our destiny is the same as theirs. Feeling losses is painful, but the pain gives way to the eternal vision of life when we know our origin and our destiny.

People will sometimes say. "Why did God allow this to happen to me?" Even though we come from the Father and are going back to the Father, the Father cannot control the free will of those who harm us on the journey. Sin causes suffering, and we see in the gospels how Jesus' heart ached when he saw the effects of sin in the world. He offered healing when he could and then offered himself in death to redeem the many misuses of freedom by humanity. God offers us his unconditional love to protect and heal us. God sent Jesus to tell us of this perfect, all-encompassing love and offer us healing from peoples' misuses of free will. Jesus gave his life to redeem us from our sins and the world's sins and heal us from the effects of those sins. Knowing that we are on this divine journey gives us security and peace from which to deal with the challenges of life.

The way we handle all of these events in life is related to how we answer the question, "Where do I come from?" I am not asking what you say to people when they ask that questions; rather, how do you answer that question within yourself? How do you perceive yourself? From what place do you approach life and meet each day? Do you think of yourself as coming from an abusive home, a non-affirming home, an alcoholic home, or a normal home? Or do you see yourself coming from the Father and going back to the Father? I invite you now to take time and ponder this question. I encourage you to open yourself to the bigger picture of your life and explore your true origin and destiny. When you are ready, we can continue to discover the deeper meanings of the "where" questions in John's gospel.

PRAYER

Jesus, your message about my divine origin gives true peace to my heart. You lived a life showing us how to live in serenity despite the effects of sin in the world. You revealed your origin and destiny and told us the we share the same. Your example of care and compassion you showed in your life tells me that you will always care for me. I honor you for that gift.

I pray now that you would allow me to feel your presence as I try to make new choices about how I perceive myself. Help me to see what you see in me. Help me to feel your divine love flowing through my whole life story. Open my eyes in a new way to the purpose for my life, and let me feel the joy you had in creating me. Give me new energy to live the fullness of my life and invite others to discover what their life could be in the awareness of your presence. Break through any blindness that exists in me so that I can clearly see the plan that you have for my life. Heal any parts of me that keep me from living out that plan completely. Thank you, Jesus, because I know this is being done. You are always faithful.

QUESTIONS FOR REFLECTION/DISCUSSION

1. What do you say when people ask, "Where do you come from? What would you like to say?

2. Have you ever experienced the type of inner healing described in this chapter? Share.

3. How would you describe your knowledge of Jesus?

4. How has your home life as a child formed your view of yourself? Are you open to changing it?

5. What part of this chapter most speaks to you?

PRACTICAL APPLICATION

Take quiet time and reflect on your true origin. Perhaps reading Psalm 139:1–14 will help you feel the Trinity love that gave you existence.

CHAPTER 3

Where Did the New Wine Come From?

On the third day there was a wedding at Cana in Galilee, and the mother of Jesus was there. Jesus and his disciples had likewise been invited to the celebration. At a certain point the wine ran out, and Jesus' mother told him, "They have no more wine." Jesus replied, "Woman, how does this concern of yours involve me? My hour has not yet come." His mother instructed those waiting on tables, "Do whatever he tells you." As prescribed for Jewish ceremonial washing, there were at hand six stone water jars, each holding fifteen to twenty gallons. "Fill those jars with water," Jesus ordered, at which they filled them to the brim. "Now," he said, "draw some out and take it to the waiter in charge." They did as he instructed them. The waiter in charge tasted the water made wine, without knowing where it had come from; only the waiters knew, since they had drawn the water. Then the waiter in charge called the groom over and remarked to him: "People usually serve the choice wine first; then when the guests have been drinking awhile, a lesser vintage. What you have done is keep the choice wine until now." Jesus performed this first of his signs at Cana in Galilee. Thus, did he reveal his glory, and his disciples believed in him.

JOHN 2:1–11

REFLECTION

As I have mentioned, the word "where" in John's gospel is significant in answering life's deeper questions. In this section, we will reflect on the story of Jesus changing the water into wine at the wedding feast in Cana. It was a marvelous miracle, but John often took these miraculous events to speak of deeper realities. At the end of the story, he mentions that this was the "first of Jesus' signs" that he performed, and the seventh sign would be the raising of Lazarus from the dead. We can see that the new wine, this choice wine, could represent the new vision of life and source of energy that Jesus came to offer. It is better than the old wine.

Jesus came to bring a new order into the world. He brought the miraculous—the world of the impossible made possible by the power of divine love. He demonstrated how to release the energy of creative love, changing what before seemed unchangeable. He brought a new power into the world, creating new realities as he once helped create the universe. He invited those who followed him to "think and act outside the box," to love with divine love, to ask for divine intervention. The gospels and Acts of the Apostles are filled with stories of how this new reality continued to be lived out through Jesus' life and the lives of his followers. He brought new wine, a new vision of reality flowing from our divine origins. History tells us of people who continued to live this life of miracles even to the present.

Notice how the word "where" directs our attention to this new divine intervention. This account says that the waiter in charge "did not know from where the new wine came." It says only the waiters knew because they were with Jesus and did what he asked them to do. The only way to know the answer to "where" is to be with Jesus. The only way to see the miracles is to "come and see," to follow where Jesus takes us and to remain with him.

This story takes us one step further into the spiritual journey. When they ran out of wine, Mary instructed the waiters to "do whatever he tells you." To see the miracles, the healings of Jesus, we need to listen to his words and to do whatever he says. In the gospel, people often saw a miracle when they did what Jesus asked them to do. In this story, Jesus said, "Fill those jars with water" and then "draw some out and take it to the waiter in charge." The directive did not make rational sense, but they did it in obedience. Because they did, they saw this marvelous miracle. In John chapter four, we read how Jesus said to the royal official, "Return home, your son will live." The man did what Jesus told him to do and started for home. On the way, he received the news that his son would live. In John chapter six, Jesus told the disciples to "get the people to recline." When they did what he said, they experienced the miraculous multiplication of loaves and fish. In chapter nine, Jesus said to the blind man, "Go, wash in the pool of Siloam." When the man did as Jesus directed, his eyes were opened. In chapter eleven, when Jesus arrived at the tomb of Lazarus, he told the people to "roll away the stone." When they did, they witnessed the raising of Lazarus from the dead. People had to do in obedience what required trust, something they normally would not do. Because they did it in response to Jesus' direction, they saw the miraculous. Mary said, "Do whatever he tells you."

These stories remind us that if we want to get the "new wine," to see the miraculous, we need to "do whatever he tells us." Letting go of our way of doing things and allowing Jesus' words to direct our lives may scare us because we often like to control things ourselves. When we think about it, we realize that Jesus is much more equipped to direct our lives than we are. He was there when we were created. We see only in a limited way, whereas Jesus sees the whole scope and purpose for our lives and the path to true inner peace. Letting go of control and intentionally listening for Jesus' direction offers us real freedom and it opens the way for stress-free living. It is a life of listening and enjoying rather than trying to control situations, and it opens the way to see miracles.

When we apply this to our emotional life, we discover that listening to Jesus' voice in our life story allows us to release feelings that we were trying to control, suppress, or medicate. Controlling or stuffing wounded feelings causes stress on our bodies and breaks down our immune system. It causes pain in our joints and tears down at our vital organs. Through prayer for inner healing, we can let go of that need to control and be freed to live in peace. This journey to inner freedom equips us to offer that gift to others. It begins with a listening spirituality, "doing whatever he tells us."

We also receive the energy and wisdom for ministry by listening to Jesus' voice and responding to his direction. We get the "new wine" by "doing whatever he tells us." We discover "where" the new wine, the healing, the transformation comes from, and we give thanks. We discover the true purpose for our life and all the gifts we need to live that purpose. We discover a deep joy from listening to the Master, the one who created us, who loved us into existence, and desires only the best for us.

To hear this healing, transforming voice, we need to turn off the noise of the world. It can be a challenge to hear the divine voice when we are bombarded with messages on our phones, computers, iPods, and televisions. It may be a challenge, but it is not impossible. It is simply a choice, a choice which is easier if we find new words to replace the old. If we take time every day to read and ponder the words in the gospels and feel the heart of Jesus and the depth of his love, the noise of the world will become less important. Our need to know the latest news diminishes when we hear the good news of healing and feel the serenity of remaining in Jesus' presence. The gospels show us the ways of Jesus, and with time, we discover the wisdom with which he spoke and related to people. His life draws us into a new way of living, a larger perspective of life, a true perspective of life. We cannot change most things on the news, but we can change the way we live and how we offer healing love to those with whom we relate. If we listen for his voice, we are equipped and empowered to "do whatever he tells us."

I believe that this is what the apostle Paul meant when he said, "Do not conform yourselves to this age but be transformed by the renewal of your mind, so that you may judge what is God's will, what is good, pleasing and perfect" (Romans 12:2). We step apart from the world to hear the eternal words from the voice of Jesus. We choose to refashion our minds to match the mind of the Creator. We choose to invite his love to refashion our wounded hearts and form them into healing hearts that are "good, pleasing and perfect." This allows us to live the fullness of life which Jesus offers us.

The inner stillness allows us to discover where the new wine, the true meaning life, comes from. It opens the way to live in the miraculous, experience inner healing and the release many of life's stresses. Whatever our past is, Jesus can make all things new if we do whatever he tells us. That is the divine message. His power is endless, and his voice is eternal. The old voices that can keep us in emotional prison are released by the voice of our Creator and redeemer. Why wouldn't we listen? Why wouldn't we want to live a life of inner peace, free of stress? Do whatever he tells you.

As we seek to listen truly for Jesus' direction in life, we will notice the need to discern which voices come from Jesus and which are our own or someone else's. Growing in discernment begins with reading and digesting the words of Jesus. We need to read all his words and watch all his actions to get an accurate picture of what he sounds like. With time, we start to get a feel for the ways of God and trust the divine love that flows over us every day, the same love that fashioned us. The more we reflect on the words and actions of Jesus, the more we will "know" his heart. We will notice the difference between his teaching and the messages of the culture, which are not really what Jesus said. We will become more aware of what voices are our own desires or our woundedness. We will notice when the voice is all about my benefit rather than the purpose Jesus has for my life. We will start to sense whether we are doing something for the approval of others or because Jesus asked us to do it. With sincere seeking and surrender, we will get a feel for the ways of Jesus and the sound of his voice. At times, "doing whatever he tells me" will be difficult, but the result will be serenity. It is sometimes helpful to have a good coach who can help us discern God's voice and support our choices while we are learning.

If we stay with Jesus and listen to his voice, we discover where we come from and where we are going. Gradually, we know where the new wine, the miraculous energy, comes from. We start to trust Jesus more and believe more completely in him. The story ends by saying that once the disciples saw this miracle, they "believed into" Jesus. They made a movement of their hearts into the heart of Jesus. It is a movement like entering into a love relationship. That heart connection is possible for us, and it grows deeper the more we listen and "do whatever he tells us." The more we connect to Jesus and feel his deep love for us, the easier it is to do whatever he tells us. We want to do what brings joy to his heart.

This movement of the heart, this new way of living for Jesus, changes our identity. We no longer see ourselves living alone but connected to the Creator of the universe. We see that what looks impossible is possible by the power of God's love for us. We approach each day with Jesus, knowing that he has a plan for us. We want to listen and follow because knowing where we are going is larger than the human challenges we meet every day. We are now part of a relationship that has eternal significance. Our identity is not all about us or what other people call us but about being a disciple, a team player in the eternal scope of life. We enjoy a love relationship, a faith relationship with the Designer of the universe, and we get to see the miraculous power of his love. We know the One from whom the "new wine" comes, and we get to drink it day after day. We know who we are because we know whose we are. This is our true identity. This is the life we were created to live.

PRAYER

Jesus, I thank you for bringing the miraculous power of your love into the world. You demonstrated great compassion and care for those in need. You listened to the Father's voice and invited us to listen as you did.

Jesus, I want to be quiet on the insideand hear your words for me. I know your voice can give true peace to my heart. Anoint me with the resolve to quiet myself every day so that your voice may truly guide my life. Open my heart to receive your healing love in all the places that still need healing. Open my mind to think as you think. Fill me with the courage to act as you would desire, to do whatever you ask of me. Help me go beyond my own rational thinking to the place where your miraculous power can change what seems impossible. Let me taste the "new wine" of your presence every day and empower me to share it with all who seek new life in you. Do not allow me to conform to this world but transform my heart and mind into the person you created me to be. Empower me to live my new identity as a transformed disciple of yours. Thank you, Jesus, for your patience with me. Thank you for continually speaking to me and loving me. Amen.

QUESTIONS FOR REFLECTION/DISCUSSION

1. How much time do you take each day to hear the voice of Jesus? Would you be willing to increase it?

2. What voices would you have to quiet to hear Jesus?

3. Do you have any time in your life when you feel you have tasted the "new wine"? Have you continued?

4. As you seek to discern the voice of Jesus, how would be different from your voice or the voice of the world?

5. How do you think your life would be different if it was directed completely by listening to Jesus?

PRACTICAL APPLICATION

Turn off your phone, computer, iPod, and television for an hour a day, and read and reflect on the gospel during that time.

CHAPTER 4

Where Do You Expect to Get This Living Water?

The hour was about noon. When a Samaritan woman came to draw water, Jesus said to her, "Give me a drink." The Samaritan woman said to him, "You are a Jew. How can you ask me, a Samaritan and a woman, for a drink?" (Recall that Jews have nothing to do with Samaritans.) Jesus replied, "If only you recognized God's gift, and who it is that is asking you for a drink, you would have asked him instead, and he would have given you living water." "Sir," she challenged him, "you do not have a bucket and this well is deep. Where do you expect to get this living water? Surely you do not pretend to be greater than our ancestor Jacob, who gave us this well and drank from it with his sons and his flocks?" Jesus replied, "Everyone who drinks this water will be thirsty again. But whoever drinks the water I give him will never be thirsty; no, the water I give shall become a fountain within him, leaping up to provide eternal life."

JOHN 4:7–14

REFLECTION

In chapter four of John's gospel, we see another double meaning of the word "where" that invites us to ponder some interesting thoughts. Jesus stops at a well near the town of Shechem to rest, and a woman comes out from the town to draw water. Jesus begins the conversation with the woman to set the stage for him to offer her a life- changing drink. Jesus lets her know that if she asks, he could give her "living water." This prompts her to ask the important question, "Where do you expect to get this living water?" The answer to the "where question" is always the same. It comes from above; it comes from the Creator.

This is the same message that we read about in chapter three when Nicodemus asks about Jesus' power to perform signs and wonders. Jesus says that you must be "born from above." You must be begotten of water and the Spirit. You must let the Spirit of God's love pour over you and wash your mind and heart of anything that is not from God. Jesus says that it is like a new birth (John 3:1–8). He describes the moment when a person discovers that they came from the Father and are going back to the Father. It is the moment a person receives the full, divine anointing available to all who accept it. And so, in this story, Jesus says to the woman, "If only you recognized God's gift, and who it is that is asking you for a drink, you would have asked him instead, and he would have given you living water" (John 4:10). He offers her a love flowing from the Father, a healing cleansing gift to transform her life.

Where do you expect to get this living water? That question opens the way for a fuller life, a life of miracles, a life of serenity. The woman first needed to ask for the water. We have free will, and God does not force us to do anything. Even though the woman did not quite understand, at least she asked. "Give me this water, sir . . ." she said. The divine, living water could begin to flow over her to heal her wounded heart and set her free. This life-giving water flowing from the Father's heart would make her new and change her life forever.

Jesus then challenges her to go and call her husband. She had been looking for love from various men, but none of them satisfied her deep longing for true love. Jesus knew that her wounded heart tempted her to attach herself to destructive relationships and Jesus knew that these unhealthy relationships were holding her back from discovering real life. Jesus does not want her to stay in a relationship that is not holy, which keeps her from living her divine purpose. She is looking for love, meaning and security in a human relationship, but Jesus is going to offer her a greater love, a healing relationship. Healthy human relationships can fill part of our longing for love, but only feeling God's deep love will completely satisfy our thirst for love.

The woman's conversation with Jesus must have changed her perception of life in a significant way. It changed her identity. She no longer saw herself as a single woman looking for love but a daughter of the Father living in love. It gave her a new view of who she really was. It gave her new courage to act as a beloved daughter. The healing water flowing over her freed her from the shame that kept her from going to the well with the other women of the town. Her experience of Jesus' love healed her "shame voice" and increased her self-esteem. It gave her the freedom and the courage to go back to the people she avoided earlier that day and invite them to "come and see" the person who told her what her life was really about. Jesus showed her from where her life came. He revealed from where the living water truly came. She was so filled that she needed to share that gift with the people of the town. She was willing to change her human relationships after entering into this divine, life-giving relationship. She was "born of water and the Spirit" flowing from "above."

Many people in the town were "thirsty" and came out to discover where they could get this living, healing water. Once they drank it, they knew who Jesus really was and who they really were. They invited him to stay with them. Once they spent time with him, they realized that he was the savior, the healer of the world. He saved them from themselves and gave them a new purpose for their lives.

Where Do I Come From?

Where do you expect to get this living water? The question comes to us and invites us to reflect on how we try to quench our deepest thirst in life. Do we quench it in human relationships? Do they often leave us less than satisfied? Jesus asked the woman to go and call her husband because he knew that her relationships were not quenching her thirst. If we are going to take in Jesus' love, we may need to look at our relationships and see if they are life-giving, if they match Jesus' way of relating. We may want to ask Jesus' love to anoint our relationships and heal the parts of them that are wounded or destructive. His unconditional love can make things new. I have often led people to experience the full power of the Holy Spirit in their life, and they told me that to live this new life in the Spirit, they needed to change who they hung out with. Their life became filled with greater serenity and peace when they allowed the living water of Jesus' love to purify and change their relationships. Some also said their marriage was renewed and deepened when they let the living water of Jesus' love flow through them. They saw themselves and their spouse in a new way.

Many of our wounds in life come from long-term relation-ships of the past. Our relationships with parents or family, especially in the early formative years, play a big part in how we see ourselves and they often affect our relationships later in life. We understand that the circumstances of our parents, while we were in the womb, can also affect our identity and our view of ourselves. Jesus' promise of living water in this story allows us to realize that we can be healed of all past events in our life. We were conceived in the perfect love of the Trinity, and that creative love of God contin-ues to pour over us to fill in the spaces where we were not loved in our life story. We do not blame those who did not love us perfectly. We are all human. What we can do is invite the perfect love of God to heal and fill those wounded and empty areas. The more healed we become, the more we will attract healthy relationships in our lives and are able to help others find healing in their relationships. This perfect love, this "flowing water," is a true gift from the Fa-ther's heart. We need only ask for it and then drink it in.

We might think about other questions: Do we keep ourselves occupied, so we do not notice our heart thirsting for something more? Do we try to quench our thirst in the pursuit of knowledge only to discover that all the study leaves us realizing that there must be bigger answers to the questions of life? Once we discover where we come from and where we are going, we realize that no earthly thing can quench our real thirst. We come to know that we must go often to the well from where the living water flows. Drinking that living water brings inner healing to our hearts and keeps us energized for our true purpose in life. It changes our identity. We do not think of ourselves as victims of bad parenting or abusive relationships but rather as reborn children of God empowered to bring others the wholeness we have received. Life looks different when we invite God's love to heal our story and forgive those who did not offer us perfect love. We discover that we can live in union with the Perfect Lover.

Once we know where the water comes from and drink in enough to heal our hearts and minds, we will invite other people to the water source. We will find that many thirsty people around us do not know where the living water comes from. We have the privilege of showing them the way. They will have to choose to "come and see," but we can make them an offer that could change their life. If they come and see, and remain with Jesus, they will come to truly know him and be willing to change their ways and follow him. It is all about choosing to discover "where" the water comes from and then letting it cleanse us and rebirth us into real life.

Jesus said that this water "shall become a fountain within us, leaping up to provide eternal life." There is an eternal dimension to this decision. Coming to receive Jesus' healing and freeing love not only enriches our life on earth but also carries the promise of life with him forever. We are empowered to share this treasure with everyone we meet. The flowing love from the heart of God never runs out and it flows over us from our origin to our destiny. Once we are awakened to receive it, our journey is filled with joy and peace that no one can take away.

PRAYER

Jesus, you have been there in my life from the moment of conception. For that, I give you thanks. You have been offering your living water, your healing presence, to me continually. You have offered me a life-giving relationship, but at times I have gotten caught up in other relationships.

Jesus, come today and fill the emptiness I feel that only your love can fill. Pour your living water of love into my heart to fill my deepest need and heal the places in me that thirst for more. Come into my relationships and purify those that are of you, and free me of those that are not in your plan. Fill me with so much of your love that it will overflow to all of the people with whom I relate. Let this well-spring of your love continue to burst forth inside me, healing and cleansing every part of me that is in need. Embolden me to carry this message of your love to the many thirsty people in the world. Thank you, Jesus, for offering to quench my deepest thirst for love. Amen.

QUESTIONS FOR REFLECTION/DISCUSSION

1. Where is your deepest thirst?

2. How do you seek to satisfy that thirst?

3. What past relationships in your life need Jesus' healing water?

4. What present relationships do you need to bring to Jesus for his healing love?

5. Who could walk with you through your story and pray with you for inner healing?

PRACTICAL APPLICATION

Spend time thanking God for the healthy, life-giving relationships in your life. Maybe you want to thank some people for walking with you to greater wholeness.

Chapter 5

Where Shall We Get Bread for These People?

A vast crowd kept following Jesus because they saw the signs he was preforming for the sick. Jesus went up the mountain and sat down there with his disciples. The Jewish feast of Passover was near; when Jesus looked up and caught sight of a vast crowd coming toward him, he said to Philip, "Where shall we buy bread for these people to eat?" (He knew well what he intended to do but he asked this to test Philip's response.) Philip replied, "Not even with two hundred days' wages could we buy loaves enough to give each of them a mouthful!"

One of Jesus' disciples, Andrew, Simon Peter's brother, remarked to him, "There is a boy here who has five barley loaves and a couple of dried fish, but what is that for so many?" Jesus said, "Get the people to recline." Even though the men numbered about five thousand, there was plenty of grass for them to find a place on the ground. Jesus then took the loaves of bread, gave thanks, and passed them around to those reclining there; he did the same with the dried fish, as much as they wanted. When they had enough, he told his disciples, "Gather up the crusts that are left over so that nothing goes to waste." At this, they gathered twelve baskets full of pieces left over by those who had been fed with the five barley loaves.

JOHN 6:2–13

REFLECTION

We continue our spiritual reflection with another story about the "living bread." It begins with the question, "Where shall we buy bread for these people to eat?" It is a similar question to all the others we have seen and it is about the larger questions of life. This one, in particular, is about how we find nurture for our lives and our ministry.

In this story, Jesus is teaching the people with the idea of drawing them into a broader view of life and his role as the "living bread." He asks Philip the question, "Where shall we buy bread for these people to eat?" He knows what he is going to do, but this is his manner of inviting people into the mystery of where real life and food are from. The discussion leads to a boy who has five loaves and a couple of dried fish. The impossibility of that amount of food feeding probably over 10,000 people sets the stage for Jesus to draw a picture of how nourishing a relationship with him could be. The multiplication of this small amount of food gave him the occasion to let people know that he was the living bread that could nurture them on their divine mission in life. The miracle itself was marvelous, but the statements Jesus made after it stretched people to decide about who Jesus was and whether they would follow him. He proclaimed himself as the bread of life and told people that unless they would "feed" on him, they would not have real life. A life in the power of the divine takes food from the divine.

Jesus answers the question of where the bread comes from by saying, "It is my Father who gives you the real heavenly bread" (John 6:32). Jesus came from the Father and is the living bread, the necessary sustenance for a life of serenity. He says that consuming his teachings, love, and direction would heal us and sustain us for an eternal relationship with him.

The story tells us that many of Jesus' disciples walked away after telling them that he was the living bread to feed their deepest needs. Jesus gave his apostles the freedom to walk away also. Peter speaks for all of them with that endearing statement, "Lord, to whom shall we go? You have the words of life, and we have come to believe; we are convinced the you are God's holy one" (John 6:68–69). They had seen Jesus' healing love change lives and they had felt his presence change their vision of themselves. They had found a purpose in life that was larger than life, and they were not going to let go of it. They had come to know where the bread came from and where it was taking them. Even though they could not explain how it happened, they knew that Jesus demonstrated power beyond their imagination. He gave them more reasons to wake up in the morning than anyone else had ever done. They understood where they came from and where they were going, and their food for the journey was a faith relationship with Jesus.

This question, "Where shall we get bread?" invites us to reflect on the question, "Where do I get bread?" Where do I get my daily nourishment? What do I consume every day? These questions can move us to think about what words, what news, what data do we let into our minds every day? We do have a choice. We do not have to listen to the news, or check social media every day. We do not have to let the computer or the television fill our minds. At times, we may need to walk away from certain discussions that distract us from our inner quiet and fill our minds with thoughts that are not life giving. We can filter what we let into our mind, heart, and spirit. If we want to have a life of inner peace, we must filter what we allow into ourselves. We must be silent. It is in the silence that we can hear the voice of Jesus.

This inner silencing and intentional filtering take discipline, but the fruits are enormous. We may also need to practice silencing our imagination to stay focused on the real food of life. If our imagination is left to move about freely in our mind, it can cause us anxiety, shame, or anger and waste time. All of this is a distraction from feeding on the living bread that Jesus gives.

In addition to filtering what we let into our mind and heart, we also need to empty ourselves of messages within our mind that are not life-giving and perhaps untrue. If we want to feed on the bread of life, the words of Jesus, we need to clear our minds of other words and other voices. We may need to dispel the untrue voices of what other people have said about us. By taking time for this inner emptying of unnecessary words and messages, we prepare ourselves for the words of Jesus to fill us and direct our lives. We allow his truth to tell us who we really are and where we are going.

This story says that many disciples walked away after Jesus taught about the real bread of life. They said Jesus' teaching was hard to accept. Everyone must make a choice. Jesus' teachings direct us in a way of acting and living that is different from the world. As Christians, we do not conform to this world. It is a challenge to live the Christian life in an environment often filled with words and behaviors that are not according to what Jesus taught. So, the question remains: Where do I get bread? What messages do I consume? Am I willing to change my thinking and actions to allow Jesus' thoughts and messages to guide and empower my life? Am I willing to stand by Jesus' teaching when others, even church leaders, go along with the culture? During challenging times, can I say with Peter, "Lord, to whom shall we go? You have the words of eternal life, and we have come to believe." Knowing our true identity as children of God empowers us to stand with Jesus no matter who else does. We must keep feeding on him, consuming his words, his teachings, his presence to carry on his divine mission for our lives.

We might go a step further. In addition to reflecting on what thoughts we allow into our mind, we might ponder what feelings we nurse that affect our heart and behavior. Are we so consumed by certain feelings that we cannot hear Jesus' voice and feel his love? Do we nurture certain assumptions about ourselves that fill us, making it impossible to feel Jesus' intense love for us and his desire to heal us? Do we harbor feelings of unforgiveness or a desire for revenge that consume us and block the message of Jesus from soaking in? Perhaps we even nurse negative assumptions about Jesus that keep us from wanting to listen to him. Maybe we were given false information about Jesus at some point in our life. If we want to have the fullness of life and be free of the weight of destructive feelings, we need to "feed" on Jesus' words which allow us to feel his deep love for us. We might begin by reading the four gospels to get a clear picture of God and his Son, Jesus. We might try to feel what Jesus was feeling and hear the deeper message he was sharing. We might feel the deep compassion he had for those in pain. To feed on him means drawing close to him and taking in his thoughts and feelings. Feeling Jesus' deep love heals our past wounds and nurtures a healthy view of ourselves. Through him, we discover our true self, our true identity.

This story also moves us to reflect on the gift of the Eucharist or Holy Communion. This account moves from saying that Jesus gave bread (verse 11), to Jesus is bread (verse 35), to Jesus is Eucharist (verses 53–56). It affirms this most important celebration in the early Christian community. It draws the crowd from just eating bread to stepping into a relationship with Jesus. It is about connecting to Jesus in a deep way so that our lives are nurtured by his living presence. The Eucharist or Communion celebrates the gift of Jesus giving himself for our redemption. It is also the time when we recommit ourselves to Jesus by offering our body and blood for his mission. We also recommit our lives to all who gather for that meal.

Participating in the weekly Eucharist was essential to be part of the early Christian community. It was a solidarity meal. They gave thanks for Jesus' commitment of his body and blood to them, and they recommitted their body and blood to him and each other. That deep commitment allowed them to withstand the persecution and empowered them to carry on Jesus' healing ministry. It remains very essential for all who wish to have the fullness of life in Jesus and demonstrate the power of his presence in the world today.

"Where shall we get bread for all these people? Jesus' question gives us much to ponder and ultimately leads us to our own question. Where do I get bread? Where do I get fed? Where do I get the energy and the power to live the Christian life and do Christian ministry? Messages keep coming to us every day, and feelings flood our hearts at times. Jesus invites us to feed on him, to consume his words each day. It is also a unique gift to gather each week at the table with Jesus and remember the love he displayed in laying down his life for us. It makes us want to do the same for him.

PRAYER

Jesus, your heart of compassion caused you to feed the many hungry people. You demonstrated your love by giving them what they needed, and you did it in a way that you could invite them to discover what "bread" they really needed. You brought them to see the unique gift of your presence to feed their deepest hunger.

I pray, Jesus, that you might open me to the many nurturing messages you have for me. Let me consume your words and take in your living presence. Help me to free myself of any thoughts or feelings that are hindrances to your thoughts for my life and your deep, healing love. Keep me faithful to your teachings despite what is going on around me. I recommit my life to you and desire to follow you wherever you lead since you do have the words of everlasting life, and I have come to believe in you. Thank you for being the living bread for us, and thank you for the sacrifice it took to be that bread.

QUESTIONS FOR REFLECTION/DISCUSSION

1. What gifts do you have that Jesus could multiply if you offered them to him?

2. What things most feed your mind each day?

3. What do you need to clear out of your mind to hear the voice of Jesus?

4. What emotions dominate your heart and prevent you from feeling Jesus' love?

5. Are there times when you are tempted to "walk away" from Jesus because his teachings are too challenging? Share.

PRACTICAL APPLICATION

Take a loaf of bread to someone and use it to begin a discussion about Jesus being the bread of life.

Chapter 6

Where Do Instructions Come From?

"Who are you, then?" the Jews asked him. Jesus answered: "What I have been telling you from the beginning. I tell the world what I have heard from him, the truthful One who sent me." They did not grasp that he was speaking to them of the Father. Jesus continued: "When you lift up the Son of Man, you will come to realize that I AM and that I do nothing by myself. I say only what the Father has taught me. The One who sent me is with me. He has not deserted me since I always do what pleases him."

JOHN 8:25-29

REFLECTION

Jesus knew that he came from the Father, and he was going back to the Father. His purpose and mission meant that he would follow the Father's will and take instructions from the Father. He says clearly, "I say only what the Father has taught me" (John 8:28). He goes on in the final chapters of this gospel to say that all that he does is directed by the Father. He says later, "I have not spoken on my own; no, the Father who sent me has commanded me what to say and how to speak" (John 12:49). Ultimately, he laid down his life to carry out the mission given to him by the Father. He allowed his life to be directed by the Father, which gave him authority and validity (John 8:14–16).

Once we realize that we came from the Father and are going back to the Father, we recognize that our instruction comes from the same source through Jesus. Jesus said, "Do you not believe that I am in the Father and the Father is in me? The words I speak are not spoken of myself; it is the Father who lives in me accomplishing his works" (John 14:10). Whatever Jesus taught came from the Father. That was the source of his authority and power. He is the mouthpiece for God's instructions. Our instructions come from Jesus' words, and our empowerment comes from his love. He says, "You will live in my love if you keep my commandments, even as I have kept my Father's commandments, and live in his love" (John 15:10). Staying aligned with Jesus' teaching gives us the anointing of his love and the power to do the kind of ministry he did. If we go outside his divine instruction, we are not assured of his authority and empowerment. The teaching of the culture or the teaching of the majority does not afford us that gift. The majority of votes does not make the teaching true, nor does it afford the divine anointing needed for miraculous ministry. Only Jesus' instructions carry the power to bring people to their ultimate purpose, eternal life in the Father's love. Jesus said, "If you live according to my teaching, you are truly my disciples; then you will know the truth, and the truth will set you free" (John 8:32).

Listening to Jesus' instructions gives us complete assurance of being on our eternal path. It is the healthiest way to live. Doing what he says allows us to witness his power and see the miraculous. Earlier, I mentioned Mary's words at Cana when they were out of wine and she said to the waiters, "Do whatever he tells you." Jesus told them, "Fill those jars with water." They saw the miracle because they obeyed Jesus' instructions. We saw this happen more often in the gospel. Early on, Jesus told the disciples to "come and see," and they saw miracles and healings when they did. Each time people did what Jesus asked, they were able to witness his miraculous power. They had not only to listen to his instructions but also to choose to submit to that instruction. Taking instruction from Jesus and teaching as he taught puts us in the stream of power that flowed through him. We can do the things he did when we are in that stream of power flowing from obedience to his word.

Where do instructions come from? We may get instructions from various people, but receiving instruction from Jesus and obeying it gives us authority not available from humans. All authority comes from the author, and Jesus is the Author of life and the one who speaks divine truth. We only have authority to teach what he taught. We do not have the authority to teach or do things that Jesus did not sanction. When we follow his instructions, it brings about a fuller, healthier life because he understands the ultimate purpose of our life. We see healings happen and even evil be driven out when we minister according to his commands. The power flows through our connection to Jesus and our obedience to his will. Once we know that we came from the Father, listening for the Father's instruction as given through Jesus is our most important task.

Listening daily and clearing our minds to hear his voice is the main work we have to do. We learn what his voice sounds like by reading and soaking in the gospels, and we learn by taking time to feel his heart. Once we know what Jesus desires, we are challenged to obey. The more we feel Jesus' love for us the easier it is to follow his direction.

Jesus' instruction is not always easy and, at times, involves living through some pain. We may get shunned, even by peers, or lose a promotion or a job. This is particularly true in a culture that pressures us to change Jesus' teaching or ridicules us for speaking his words. During my years in training to be a pastor, some instructors taught that the healings of Jesus never happened and that he did not rise from the dead. They were influenced by the teachings coming from the Enlightenment of the 19th century. These influences have kept the healing ministry suppressed in many churches. I had witnessed many healings through prayer and often spoke of Jesus' power and desire to heal people today. I received some ridicule, but I had come to know that being true to Jesus was the way to know true joy and peace. Once we know our origin and destiny, we realize that faithfulness to him is the only way to live.

Jesus' messages to us may come in many forms. We may read a scripture passage and sense it is a word to us for that day. We may get an idea in our quiet time, which seems to be from Jesus. A message like that was the origin of two of my books. I sometimes sense that it is a good time to call someone, and when I do, they often needed a call, and the conversation then felt like it was divinely directed. We may feel a call to pray for healing for someone, and when we ask if there is something for which they need prayer, we discover why we had the notion. I believe Jesus sends us messages often, and the more we know him and seek to follow his way, the more we will accept and act on those messages. When we are obedient to Jesus' message for ministry, we receive the energy and anointing to do as he asks.

Jesus offers us a precious image to let us know that our connection to him is the source of true life and ministry. He says, "I am the vine, and you are the branches. The one who lives in me and I am in him, will produce abundantly, for apart from me you can do nothing" (John 15:5). The energy to do the works of Jesus comes from unity with him. Cut off from him, we not only lose our authority but also lose our energy and anointing for the miraculous. The fruitfulness of our life and ministry is dependent on staying connected tightly to him. He gives us all that we need to live a life of inner peace, find healing, and arrive safely at our ultimate destiny. The way home gets easier the more we listen to his instruction and receive all the love he lavished on us. Once we know the way, we can invite others onto the path and show them the avenues for receiving his love.

PRAYER

Jesus, you demonstrated a faithfulness to the Father's instruction. You showed us the power flowing from that faithfulness. Your life also exemplified the deep love the Father in heaven has for us and the divine desire to have us arrive at our final destination.

I pray for the strength and wisdom to follow your instructions throughout my life. Keep me on the path of faithful surrender to whatever you ask of me. Anoint me with a deep awareness of your constant love flowing over me and through me, bringing healing and the empowerment I need for my calling in life. Give me discernment to know which directives are from you, and help me dispel those that are not. Fill me with courage to act as you would act in all situations so that my life will speak your message of faithful love. Thank you, Jesus, for revealing the Father's will and the love that created me. Thank you for being faithful to the Father, even at the cost of your life. I thank you for the fruits of your redeeming love, and I commit myself to follow your way. Amen.

QUESTIONS FOR REFLECTION/DISCUSSION

1. How do we make sure we teach only what Jesus has taught us?

2. What are the times you find it most difficult to obey Jesus?

3. Have you ever experienced something miraculous when you did what Jesus asked you to do?

4. Share a time when you heard someone speak with the authority of Jesus. How did it make you feel?

5. How do you stay connected to the Vine? How do you take in the flow of Jesus' energy?

PRACTICAL APPLICATION

Write down some messages you have received from Jesus. Reflect on how they have guided your life.

Chapter 7

Where Do You Serve From?

> *Jesus, fully aware that he had come from God and was going to God, the Father who had handed everything over to him, rose from the meal and took off his cloak. He picked up a towel and tied it around himself. Then he poured water into a basin and began to wash his disciples' feet and dry them with the towel he had around him.*
>
> JOHN 13:3–5

REFLECTION

These reflections on where we come from and where we are going lead us to the ultimate source of energy for a life of inner peace and an impactful ministry. In one of his last gestures, Jesus demonstrates that true service flows from knowing our true identity, origin, and destiny. Jesus, "aware that he had come from God and was going to God," does something that only a servant in that culture would have done. He could do this humble act, this "servant's work," because he did not care what other people thought of it. He only cared what the Father desired. He knew who he was. His service flowed from his identity. He showed his disciples and us that true servant ministry flows from our true identity. What our ministry looks like to others is not our concern when we are directed and empowered by God.

Jesus did not need to please anyone but the Father. He did not have to look good in anyone else's eyes. He did not go after personal gain. Jesus only did what he was directed to do. He could humbly submit to the Father's will because he knew who he was. True humility flows from knowing our true identity.

Christian humility involves the surrender of our pride and acceptance of Jesus' guidance. It is a turning away from our need to look good. It is simply doing what Jesus asks. It is a decision to listen to the Master's voice rather than the voice of our culture or the messages of our wounded inner voices. The voice of the fear of what others will think, the voice of possibly being shamed for our actions, or the voice of not being good enough can hold us back from living or speaking as Jesus taught. These all give way to the voice of Jesus when we know our true identity. In this story, Jesus models a humble act of kindness and care for his disciples without regard for how he might look. He demonstrates the core of true ministry, namely, knowing his origin and destiny. Then he was prepared to listen for the Father's voice. This voice guided his actions and his teaching.

This gesture of Jesus invites us to consider the reason why we do the things we do. Are our life and ministry influenced by what other people think, or are they directed by the discerned voice of the Creator? Do we teach as Jesus taught no matter what the culture says? Do we do what Jesus did because he is asking it of us? The way we act and how we carry out our ministry has much to do with how we perceive ourselves. Through my years in ministry, I have watched Christian leaders turn away from the gospel message because someone would be offended if they spoke as Jesus would speak. I have talked with church leaders who would not get involved in the healing ministry because they did not want their peers to ridicule them. I understand the pain of ridicule, but if we know where we came from and where we are going, if we know who we are in Jesus' plan, that pain does not stop our ministry.

I have been inspired by people in ministry who know who they are and whose they are. They speak with clarity and conviction because they know their roots and destiny. They are like the leaders in the early church who taught the message of Jesus despite the consequences for themselves. They remind me of Peter standing before the Sanhedrin proclaiming Jesus' message of salvation without backing down (Acts 4–5). He risked his life to be faithful to the Master. They remind me of the apostle Paul teaching and preaching with divine authority without regard for his comfort or safety. Their ministry changed lives because they allowed Jesus' voice to change their lives. They did not focus on the consequences but on the divine mission entrusted to them. "Jesus, fully aware that he had come from God and was going back to God," washed the disciples' feet and demonstrated for them the power of knowing his true identity. That is the place from which we can do life-transforming ministry. We start with where we came from and where we are going, and then we invite Jesus to heal the inner wounds that keep us from living our true identity.

I have worked with many people who are so caught up in pleasing someone else that they never live their lives. They never discover who they are because they do not start with where they came from and where they are going. Their life was controlled by another's response rather than the voice of their Creator. They lived with an interior sadness because intuitively, they knew they were not the person they were meant to be. Through prayer for healing the child within, many were able to release the false voices that controlled their life and hear Jesus' voice affirming their goodness and true identity as sons and daughters of the Father. They started to become the person they were created to be. They discovered inner freedom and a deep serenity which brought great joy. As they experienced inner healing, they changed any behavior in their life that was not in keeping with Jesus' teaching. They often moved into ministry without a need for reward or concern about what other people thought. They humbly offered their gifts to honor the Master. They could "wash other's feet" because they had been washed clean on the inside.

Where do we serve from; where do we minister from? Where do we draw energy for the challenges of doing the work that Jesus calls us to do? This story invites us to reflect on who we really are and what is important. It is empowering both for our lives and our ministry. It demonstrates an interior place from which we can live with deep, inner peace and where we can do authentic Christian ministry. It takes us to the core of who we are in God's eyes, and it frees us from the control of others who have not yet discovered their true identity. It leaves us free from the voices of the culture that often focus on personal gain and pleasure or false freedom outside of the Master's calling.

Jesus' gesture of washing the disciple's feet shows us why it is important to discover our true identity. It demonstrates the value of receiving inner healing prayer to quiet the voices that otherwise skew our ministry and our lives. It encourages us to continually re-member where we come from and where we are going. This gives us an inner clarity from which we can serve others as Jesus did and nobody can take that away from us.

PRAYER

Jesus, your example of humble service inspires me to serve as you did. Your inner strength to carry out the Father's will with con-sistent focus and constant faithfulness invites me to do the same. Your awareness of where you came from and where you were go-ing gave you interior empowerment for ministry.

I pray, Jesus, for the clarity of vision with which you lived. I ask you for the courage to stay free of the temptation to turn away from your will because of what others might say. Keep me constantly aware of your healing and empowering love so that I will follow your direction in all circumstances. Anoint my life with the inner peace which sustained your life. Help me to stay humble in serving you, knowing that all I am and all I do is for your glory. Thank you for creating me and showing me how to live a life of serenity and peace. Thank you, too, for the hope of living in your presence forever. Amen.

QUESTIONS FOR REFLECTION/DISCUSSION

1. What things come to mind as you reflect on this story of Jesus washing the disciple's feet?

2. What voices most control or influence your life?

3. What voices would you like to change to have greater inner peace? Where would you begin?

4. As you grow in hearing the Master's voice, how might your ministry change?

5. What things might help you stay humble as you go about your life activities?

PRACTICAL APPLICATION

Write down why you do the things you do and why you say the things you say. Reflect on how it is related to your true identify?

CHAPTER 8

Where Do You Remain?

Jesus said, "In my Father's house there are many dwelling places; otherwise how could I have told you that I was going to prepare a place for you, and then come back to take you with me, that where I am you may also be."

JOHN 14:2-3

REFLECTION

The final "where" in John's gospel is an endearing promise. Jesus expressed his enduring love for his disciples by using the words that a man of his time would use to propose marriage to his beloved. He said to them at their last meal together, "In my Father's house there are many dwelling places; otherwise, how could I have told you that I was going to prepare a place for you, and then come back to take you with me, that where I am you also may be" (John 14:2-3).

"That where I am, you also may be." Those words express Jesus' deep love and desire for us. They tell us that the only thing that really matters in life is that where the Father and Jesus are, we are also. It is the place of perfect love. It is where we were conceived. It is the center of the Trinity where perfect love creates and restores life. It is our origin and our destiny. Jesus' desire is that where he is, we are, every day of our lives. He said, "As the Father has loved me, so I have loved you. Remain in my love" (John 9:15). It is the promise of divine intimacy and the assurance that we are precious to God.

The gospel has shown us that remaining in Jesus is where we get our true identity and a true picture of what is important. This is the place where the new wine, the new anointing, comes from. This is where the flowing, healing water comes from. This is the place where the true bread comes from. This is the place where true instruction comes from. This is the only place to be if we want to know real joy and the fullness of life. We can live in the place every day. It is accessible to us and available for the asking. If we feel like we are not living in that place because of past behaviors that are not as Jesus taught, he invites us to confess them and receive his abundant mercy. If we do not live this life of deep unity with Jesus because we are afraid of what other people will think, I can tell you that it only matters what Jesus thinks. If we do not live with his deep peace because of wounded memories or difficult traumas, Jesus invites us to allow his healing love to flow through our whole story. If we have never experienced Jesus' deep love for us, he waits for us to find an environment where we can make a full commitment to him and receive his perfect love, his Holy Spirit. Jesus wants us to live where he lives. He wants us to breathe in his love every moment of every day.

Jesus promises that we can ultimately end in that place of the Father's perfect love. He tells us we can get a taste of that place all along life's journey if we "come and see"; that is, we move out of our small vision of life and discover that we came from the Father and we are going back to the Father. If we "come and see" what Jesus said and how he lived we can experience heavenly, divine joy on earth to encourage us on the journey. We can taste the healing energy, the new wine, the living water flowing from the heart of the Father to us. We can eat the bread of life and feel the deep love that Jesus expressed when he gave his body and blood for our redemption. We can hear the words of life that Jesus spoke, which pull us out of this world into a world of miracles and new life. And so we are left to ponder the words, "where do we remain?"

Jesus offered some final words to his disciples before his death. He said, "Remain in me as I do in you" (John 15:3b). The word "remain" here is the same word used in the first question, "Where do you stay (remain)?" The disciples had to find out where Jesus stayed so they could remain with him and he could remain with them. At the end of their journey, he invites them to remain in him as he does in them. The word takes on a new meaning. It moved from meaning a physical presence to a deeper remaining presence in the heart. It expresses the eternal, divine connection.

The precious good news of this message is that we can remain in Jesus every day. We can live in the divine presence. We are encircled by divine, unconditional love continually, and all we need to do is receive it. We can live consciously aware of this Holy love, this Holy Spirit, every moment of every day. It is the place Jesus has invited us to live. This presence makes all the cares of the world much smaller. This holy presence gives us the power to bring healing in Jesus' name and the ability to forgive others and forgive ourselves. It gives us the ability to encourage and affirm the good in others. Remaining in Jesus is possible because Jesus remains in us, and we live in the middle of perfect love. We are from the perfect love of the Father, and we are going back to the perfect love of the Father. The closer we stay to Jesus and his words, the more our life journey is soaked in love.

Because many things in our world distract us, or tempt us, or pull at us, we need to intentionally choose to remain with Jesus. Some people begin each day with at least fifteen minutes of quiet time reflecting on Jesus' words and worshipping him. Some end the day giving thanks and pondering how Jesus was present to them that day. Many people who desire this fullness of life begin each week by celebrating Holy Communion, remembering Jesus' sacrifice of himself for them and recommitting their body and blood to him. Some gather with other Christians to study the Scripture or pray with each other for healing. Some walk and talk with Jesus as they go. Being with other Christians who know the heart of Jesus and talking about his love can be very helpful in feeling Jesus' love every day. Whatever helps us remain in the divine presence is a very important thing to do. It is the place Jesus wants us to be.

At their final meal together, Jesus offered the disciples one final gift. He said, "Peace is my farewell to you, my peace is my gift to you; I do not give it as the world gives peace" (John 14:27). True inner peace is one thing we cannot get from the world. We cannot find our true identity from the world; it comes from a heart connection to our Creator, our Redeemer. It comes from a connection to our divine origin and destiny and from listening to the Divine voice and then following that voice.

Where do you come from? Where do you remain? Where are you going? These are the most important questions we have to answer to discover a peaceful, meaningful and fulfilling life. The gospel of John points us to the One who can direct us to that kind of life. He is "the way, the truth and the life" (John 14:6). These reflections give us a chance to think about how we answer those questions and where our life is going. No matter what circumstances we were born into or what environment we encountered early in life, the Father's love was there first, and the Father's love will be there at the end. Jesus's love is available to handle the challenges, heal the wounds, forgive the sins, and to empower the next steps. The Holy Spirit encompasses us and pervades our whole being. We start in Love, we live in Love and we end in Love. That is where we find our true identity.

PRAYER

Jesus, thank you for your profound message to us. It is evident that you desire only the best for us and have given us a way to receive this abundant, miraculous life. You came into the world to offer us this gift. Thank you for the sacrifice that opened this opportunity for us.

I pray, Jesus, help me consciously to remain in your presence every minute of every day. Help me live in that holy place of your

Father's perfect love and feel the joy of that place. I ask you to pour a fresh anointing of your Holy Love over me right now that I may be cleansed of all that is not of you and that I may be empowered to offer your love to the people I encounter. Flood my mind with your wisdom and words of direction for my life and flood my heart with the Peace that passes all understanding. I want to remain in you as you remain in me. I want to be where you are. Thank you for your life-giving presence and for introducing me to the Father's perfect love. Thank you for teaching me of my true identity found in you. Amen.

QUESTIONS FOR REFLECTION/DISCUSSION

1. What would you need to do to remain consciously in the Father's love every day?

2. What question has most spoken to you through this journey?

3. What changes in your life might you make because of these reflections?

4. Who would you like to invite into this life of peace, residing in the Father's love?

5. Where do you come from, and where are you going?

PRACTICAL APPLICATION

Live your life every day as if you know that you came from the Father and that you are going back to the Father.

About the Author

Rev. Paul Feider was born and raised in Wisconsin. His preparation for priesthood included two years of college at the University of Innsbruck, Austria. He completed his Masters of Divinity degree in Milwaukee and was ordained in 1977.

Rev. Paul has spent his 45 years of priestly ministry passionately leading people in his community and surrounding area to a deep love for God, teaching about the power of God's word and bringing God's healing touch to many. He has traveled to Australia, Europe, Guatemala, Kenya, Uganda, Madagascar, and nationally, teaching and ministering God's healing love.

Rev. Paul has written six books entitled:

The Christian Search for Meaning in Suffering

Paul's Letters for Today's Christian

Journey to Inner Peace

Sacraments: Encountering the Risen Lord

Resting in the Heart

Healing Miracles in Acts of the Apostles

In 1979, he became an active member of the Association of Christian Therapists (www.actheals.org). In 1996, he became a member of the Order of St. Luke (www.OSLToday.org), a national organization dedicated to equipping God's people with the healing ministry of Jesus. He has served as president of their board and continues to serve on the board. He is also on the National Board of Directors for Christian Healing Ministries (www.christianheal-ingmin.org), directed by Judith MacNutt.

Rev. Paul retired six years ago from serving as pastor of St. John's Church and Center for Inner Peace in New London, Wisconsin. He was able to initiate growth in the church by the power of the Holy Spirit to the point where they went from nearly closing to needing a new church building. He designed the new church and was the main builder for that structure. St. John's was a central place for teaching, worship, and healing ministry for his last 18 years as a pastor. From this place, Rev. Paul taught the School for Christian Healing, the Spiritual Enrichment Seminars and weekly bible studies in addition to offering many opportunities for healing prayer.

Rev. Paul is married to Julie, who is s Licensed Professional Counselor. He has a fire in his heart for inviting people into the heart of God. His gifts of preaching, teaching, praying, and administrating have been anointed by the Holy Spirit to bring many people to greater wholeness and inner peace.